YOU CAN TELL YOU'RE A YORKER
IF . . .

by Curvin Diffenderfer.   Illustrated by Joshua Biden.

WINEMILLER PRESS
YORK, PA

Library of Congress Catalog Card Number: 96-61923

ISBN 0-9655877-1-1 (pbk.)

Winemiller Press books are available at special discounts when purchased in bulk for premiums and sales promotions as well as for fund-raising or educational use. Special editions or book excerpts can also be created to specification. For details, contact Winemiller Press at the address below.

Winemiller Press
2625 Winemiller Lane
York, PA 17404
Manufactured in the United States of America

First printing December 1996
Second printing January 1997

DEDICATION

This book is dedicated to the immigrants who left Germany in the 18th century and found their way to the New World and to York, Pennsylvania. It was their hard work, sense of community, and thrift which are probably the major reasons why York is the beautiful and prosperous place it is today.

It was also this tightly knit community which was the defining force in creating "Yorkness" -- the culture of York -- without which this book would not have been possible.

CONTENTS

YORK is not just a place, it's a frame of mind. It's not just a county, it's a history. It's not just one small part of "Pennsylvania Dutch Country", it's . . . well . . . it's different! Residents of York have a history of being a very close-knit people with a predominant ethnic group (German) and with many of their ancestors coming from the same province in Germany. York has developed its own idiosyncrasies, language, lifestyle, eating habits, and perhaps even driving habits.

Lifelong residents don't always know that they have this distinct culture and people relocating to York sometimes don't understand the culture into which they have moved. Yorkers are not always helpful to these newcomers because Yorkers take York for granted.

This book is an attempt to provide the help needed in order to understand and thrive in the York culture. Special emphasis is given to those moving in so that they will have a smoother transition. (**NOTE TO NEWCOMERS:** Please remember, while your transition will be made smoother by reading this book, you will **never** be a Yorker.)

The book is also a useful yardstick for those who are lifelong residents of the area. Since Yorkers often take their "Yorkness" for granted, many times they do not know what being from York really means. This book can help these natives see just how "York" they are and even determine if they are "hard-core" Yorkers.

YOU CAN TELL YOU'RE A YORKER IF . . . you can see yourself in this book.

YOU CAN TELL YOU'RE A YORKER IF . . .

LIFESTYLE

Yorkers have a definite lifestyle. They tend to be frugal, meticulous, and conservative. As a result they tend to have healthy savings accounts, keep great lawns, and vote Republican. They love their vacations and spend them where there is either sand or deer. Yorkers don't schedule any social events on the first Monday after Thanksgiving or during the entire month of July.

When they work, however, they work hard. Yorkers tend to rise early, even if their job doesn't demand it. Want a meeting? Do it at breakfast. Yorkers tend to look down their noses at late risers, unless they work third shift.

YOU CAN TELL YOU'RE A YORKER IF . . .

You belong to a golf or bowling league sponsored by your Sunday School.

You shop more at Hills than at Hecht's.

You have a scraggly beard and you're not a hippie.

You sit on a curb and watch at least two different Halloween Parades.

Every summer you go to Ocean City, Maryland for two weeks of laying out.

YOU CAN TELL YOU'RE A YORKER IF . . .

You don't use turn signals because you know where *you're* going.

You think that Route 30 has the worst traffic in the Western Hemisphere.

You think that the York Fair is the greatest fun you can have in York during the entire year.

Your name is Clair . . . and you're a man.

You leave your lawn chairs along the Halloween Parade route two days in advance -- and they are never stolen.

YOU CAN TELL YOU'RE A YORKER IF . . .

You actually watch the Golf Channel and the Weather Channel.

Someone gives you a plant and you say, "I can't thank you!"

You own a motor home.

You don't have a friend next door, she's a "neighbor lady."

You don't "trick or treat" on Halloween night -- your town sets "trick or treat" night on a day other than Halloween.

YOU CAN TELL YOU'RE A YORKER IF . . .

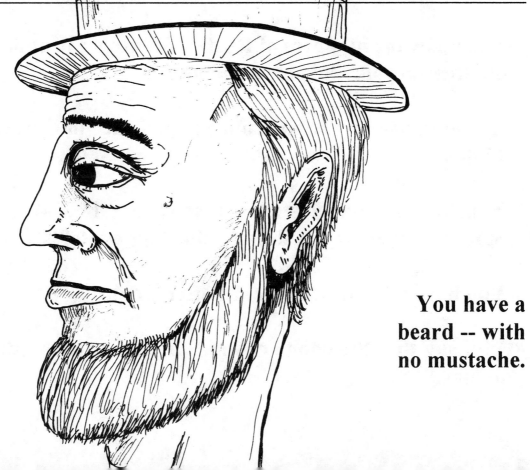

You have a
beard -- with
no mustache.

YOU CAN TELL YOU'RE A YORKER IF . . .

You know the numbers of Rusty Wallace's car and you fly his number on your flagpole on Sundays.

All your ancestors came from one province in Germany in the 1740's.

You have a bumper sticker that reads "If God isn't a Penn State fan, then why is the sky blue and white?"

You have a hunting camp in Potter County.

You say that the odor around Spring Grove is "the smell of money."

FOOD

The food eaten by Yorkers generally has two things in common: pork and cholesterol. Real York food was developed from centuries of living on farms. It tastes good; it's made from those animals which German farmers raised; and it is nourishing. Farming as the source of common York foods has been modified by the Maryland and Chesapeake Bay connection which has added seafood, particularly crabs and oysters, to the diet of Yorkers.

Much of traditional York food can not be described to non-Yorkers

YOU CAN TELL YOU'RE A YORKER IF . . .

without them wincing just a little. Most Americans are familiar with sausage in a casing, but a description of hog maw, a peek at scrapple, a list of the different parts of a hog which Yorkers consume, and the use of lard in fasnachts are enough to cause these non-Yorkers to shake their heads.

It has been said that the Yorkers' eating habits haven't changed in 200 years even though most Yorkers don't work those long hours on a farm to burn off the calories consumed. But then, as a Yorker once observed, "When I had my heart attack, the Doctor didn't say that it was caused by eating hog maw!"

YOU CAN TELL YOU'RE A YORKER IF . . .

Variety in a meal means switching from mashed potatoes to scalloped potatoes.

You like raisin gravy, pineapple gravy, milk gravy, and yellow gravy.

You go to a restaurant for breakfast at least three times a week.

You can take apart a crab and eat all the meat in about 58 seconds.

You cook "filling" in your turkey, not "stuffing" and certainly not "dressing."

YOU CAN TELL YOU'RE A YORKER IF . . .

You like soft shell crab sandwiches with their little legs dangling off the bread.

You put stewed tomatoes on top of macaroni and cheese.

You make "deer bologna" from your venison.

You know what "pot pie" is.

You go to Oyster Feeds and line up for "raws."

You think that there is no such thing as "bad" cholesterol.

YOU CAN TELL YOU'RE A YORKER IF . . .

You don't eat meat
unless it's in
a casing.

LANGUAGE

Yorkers have their own slang, dialect, and verbal mannerisms. Like natives of any area of the country, however, they often don't know that they use these "idioms". Much of the York dialect is a result of its "Dutch" heritage and close knit community. A Yorker once related that when she was in Missouri, a clerk asked, "Are you from York?" The clerk herself was originally from York and she had recognized the patterns and phrases which make York distinct.

YOU CAN TELL YOU'RE A YORKER IF . . .

Many "Yorkisms" are words, phrases, or speech patterns brought by German settlers and modified in York over the years. Other Yorkisms are simply regional idioms while still others originate with the original Scotch-Irish settlers of the County.

This book is not a history of York's language and we're not here to determine where these distinctive phrases came from or what their roots are -- we're here to enjoy them!

YOU CAN TELL YOU'RE A YORKER IF . . .

You tend to add an apostrophe when making words plural, such as "Waitress's wanted", "Condo's for sale", or "Free Kitten's."

You go to an O's ball game in "Bawlamer."

You don't clean your house, you "rett it up."

From York, you go "up" to Hanover.

Things aren't "great", they're "Wonderful Good."

YOU CAN TELL YOU'RE A YORKER IF . . .

The verb "to be" isn't in your vocabulary. You say:
    "This car needs fixed";
    "This house needs cleaned"; or
    "The grass needs cut."

Instead of saying, "It's raining cats and dogs!" you say, "It's really making rain!"

When predicting wet weather, you say, "They want rain."

You are a waitress and you say, "Can I take your order awhile?"

YOU CAN TELL YOU'RE A YORKER IF . . .

When you leave
a room, you
"outen the lights."

YOU CAN TELL YOU'RE A YORKER IF . . .

You pronounce "All" and "Oil" the same.

The plural of "You" is "Youse" ("Youns" is a Pittsburgh phrase which sometimes sneaks in the back door).

You say "Close the door once", or even close the door "oncet."

Your answering machine says, "Please <u>let</u> a message", not "Please <u>leave</u> a message."

YOU CAN TELL YOU'RE A YORKER IF . . .

You use "wooder" to "warsh" clothes.

"BETTER HOMES AND GARDENS"

Travel through York County on the first day of May and you will be greeted by what seems to be a paradise. You will be amazed by the beauty of the flowering shrubs, flowers, and bulbs gracing the houses of York. The lawns are meticulous, and the houses well maintained. This sight will be repeated on narrow country roads, in downtown areas of cities and boroughs, or in the ubiquitous suburban drives. York homes are well kept -- perhaps compulsively so. Lawns and flowers are prized and even modest homes are often landscaped in a breathtaking manner.

YOU CAN TELL YOU'RE A YORKER IF . . .

This beauty does not come easily or cheaply, however. Lawn equipment dealers and plant nurseries are kept busy, while Yorkers themselves work very long hours to get their house and lawn looking just the way they want it.

Historically, clay was more plentiful than wood, and most York houses built between 1800 and 1980 are made of brick. In fact, it was only with the rapid population growth and higher building material costs of the 1980's that wood and then vinyl siding began replacing brick in most houses in York -- a trend which Yorkers are *not* excited about.

YOU CAN TELL YOU'RE A YORKER IF . . .

Each time you cut your grass, you do it twice. The first cut follows a line on a diagonal with the street, then the second cut is at a 90 degree angle from the first cut. Then, the next time the grass needs cut, you reverse the angles so that the angle of the cutting path is different each time.

You own an electric lawn edging machine.

You think that any house is poorly made if it isn't made of brick.

You use a lawn service.

YOU CAN TELL YOU'RE A YORKER IF . . .

You use at least $100 worth of electricity for your Christmas decorations. You also put up a lawn full of Halloween decorations; fill your trees with Easter Eggs; and put up your flag on every holiday.

When you trim your trees, you don't thin the branches, you "top" the trees so that when the leaves are gone the branches look like stubby fingers sticking into the air.

YOU CAN TELL YOU'RE A YORKER IF . . .

You own at least two lawn mowers -- one a riding mower and one a self-propelled walk behind mower. You might even own a back-up for one of these.

You sweep the street in front of your house.

Your house has arborvitae along the foundation.

Every plate in your house is Pfaltzgraff . . . and most are "seconds."

YOU CAN TELL YOU'RE A YORKER IF . . .

MISCELLANEOUS

There are many other things which make a Yorker unique. If there weren't, there wouldn't be enough to fill this book! These traits, cultural idiosyncrasies, habits, or whatever you call them can't be categorized or put in a box. These traits are noticed at once by new residents in the area, while natives take them for granted. they are not good or bad, they are just . . . York.

YOU CAN TELL YOU'RE A YORKER IF . . .

Your wife and daughter are blondes.

You don't live in a Third World country, but you still "go to market" each week.

Your name is Diffenderfer, Dunklebarger, Dittenhafer, or Deardorff.

Your name is "Myers". If your name is "Meyers", you are *not* from York.

You very seldom "cross over" the Susquehanna River to Lancaster County.

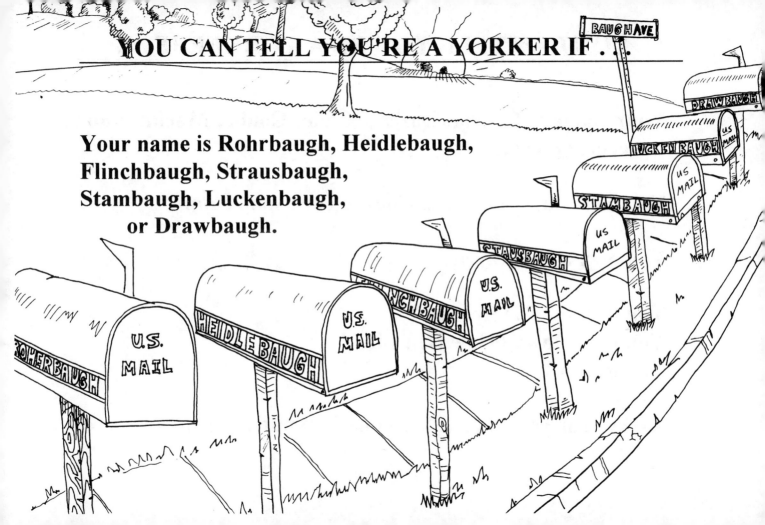

YOU CAN TELL YOU'RE A YORKER IF . . .

Your name is Rohrbaugh, Heidlebaugh, Flinchbaugh, Strausbaugh, Stambaugh, Luckenbaugh, or Drawbaugh.

YOU CAN TELL YOU'RE A YORKER IF . . .

Your name is Curvin, Dorcas, Clair, Goldie, Marlin, Fairy, Laverne, or Treva.

You met your spouse at a chicken corn soup supper.

You own a motorcycle.

You live in "The Brogue."
You live "down below Red Lion."
You live in Yoe.

Every year you go to at least one Fireman's Carnival.

YOU CAN TELL YOU'RE A YORKER IF . . .

WINTER

Winter in York is tough -- not because the weather is so bad, but because Yorkers just don't like it! Instead, Yorkers like humidity, sand, blistering heat! Anything but cold and snow.

Luckily for Yorkers, the area has probably the mildest winters and the hottest summers in the State, as well as the most humid climate. Unfortunately, sometimes it snows and Yorkers . . . well, Yorkers aren't real good with snow.

Sometimes Yorkers have to face . . . **WINTER!**

YOU CAN TELL YOU'RE A YORKER IF . . .

When you hear the word "snow", you have an uncontrollable urge to run out and buy toilet paper, milk, and bread.

You don't like snow because . . . well, it's just too messy!

You blow or throw snow into the street so that it doesn't create a problem in your lawn.

You own at least one snow blower.

You shovel your drive at 4:00 AM then curse the snow plow when it fills your driveway with snow at 5:00 AM.

YOU CAN TELL YOU'RE A YORKER IF . . .

You don't go "sledding" or "sleighing", you go "coasting."

After an ice storm, things get "slippy."

Each year you mow your grass at least once while it's snowing.

You wear shorts . . . in January.

During a storm, you call the municipal offices and tell them that you are a volunteer fireman, doctor, heating fuel delivery man -- anything to get a snow plow to your street.

"HARD CORE" YORKERS

Believe it or not, there are "hard core" Yorkers who amaze even life-long residents. These people can still speak Dutch in complete sentences and are fonts of knowledge about all the things discussed in this book.

Hard core Yorkers generally live in the small towns which dot the York countryside, and they often still have connections with agriculture. They go ordinary Yorkers one better since they think that run-of-the-mill, life-long Yorkers are too trendy!

HARD CORE YORKERS

You actually make your own hog maw.
"   "   "   "   "   scrapple.
"   "   "   "   "   fasnachts.

At least one of your grandparents didn't speak English until first grade . . . and she was a 7th generation American.

When you served in World War II, they used you as a translator to talk to captured German soldiers.

YOU CAN TELL YOU'RE A YORKER IF . . .

You own a riding lawn mower, a self-propelled push mower, a leaf blower, a gasoline powered weed eater, an electric lawn edging machine, at least one snow blower, and a small chain saw.

YOU CAN TELL YOU'RE A YORKER IF . . .

You've only been into the City of York twice . . . and you've lived in York County all your life.

You've slaughtered a hog at least twice.

You have either grown tobacco or worked in a cigar factory.

You always eat pork and sauerkraut on New Year's Day.

You always eat fasnachts on Fat Tuesday.

You don't eat meat unless it's in a casing.

YOU CAN TELL YOU'RE A YORKER IF . . .

Your favorite saying is, "But we've always done it that way!"

GUIDE FOR NEWCOMERS

There are a great many people moving to York each day. York's weather, access to jobs, and beauty of the countryside draw new residents like magnets. However, these newcomers don't always understand Yorkers or their culture. This lack of knowledge can reduce job opportunities, give a bad first impression, and cause your children to be laughed at in school -- often causing permanent psychological damage.

Presented for your enlightenment are a few phrases which, if used judiciously, might save the newcomer from needless embarrassment.

YOU CAN TELL YOU'RE A YORKER IF . . .

"I'll get your water awhile." This phrase or some variation is often used by waitresses, sales clerks, or someone waiting on you. It does not mean that they will help for "awhile" and then stop. It means that they will perform the task in question until the rest of the job can be done, such as you making up your mind about what meal you will order.

Do *not* ask the Yorker if their statement means that they are going to stop getting the water in the middle of the task. You will be given a stare meaning, "What planet is this Bozo from?", and the Yorkers in your group won't know what you are referring to, thus branding yourself as a dullard in their eyes.

YOU CAN TELL YOU'RE A YORKER IF . . .

"This car needs fixed." The verb "to be" is often thought to be superfluous to a Yorker. Newcomers will often say that "the car needs <u>to be</u> fixed," but don't try to correct the Yorker or even chuckle at their colloquialism. They don't realize that it is colloquial and your explanation will be too long and they will think that you are a dullard.

You will also notice that occasional headlines in local papers will use this sentence structure, such as **"Councilman declares that truck needs fixed"**. It is often unknown if the individual writing the headline is a Yorker or if he is an outsider who is poking fun at Yorkers.

YOU CAN TELL YOU'RE A YORKER IF . . .

"The beer is all." Resist the urge to ask, "all what?". This statement simply means that there is no more beer. Remember, being frugal people, Yorkers do not use extra words when they feel they are unnecessary. To add the word "gone" after "all" would be using a superfluous word. However, if you do ask, "All what?", you will be given a blank stare and be thought of as a dullard.

YOU CAN TELL YOU'RE A YORKER IF . . .

Dandelions. Don't have them growing in your yard or risk a visit from a delegation representing your neighborhood. Your neighbors will all be using a combination of chemicals and elbow grease to assure that there are no dandelions in their yards (see *Better Homes and Gardens*). If you have dandelions, you will be harboring a menace which will cost your neighbors money and sweat -- not a good reputation to have in your neighborhood.

YOU CAN TELL YOU'RE A YORKER IF . . .

"FASNACHTS"

DID YOU KNOW? 75% of the fasnachts made in America are eaten in York County. The rest are thrown away.

YOU CAN TELL YOU'RE A YORKER IF . . .

DID YOU KNOW? It has been shown that eating one fasnacht will add 80 points to your cholesterol count within 15 minutes.

DID YOU KNOW? The proper way to make fasnachts is to use pure lard. So-called "modern" fasnacht-makers use a vegetable oil. These cooks are sneered at by hard core Yorkers.

USES FOR SURPLUS FASNACHTS:

a. To grease skids.
b. To "call in" crows.
c. To make you feel happy that you will be fasting for Lent.
d. To prop doors open.

YORK QUIZ

Now that you've read all about Yorkers, including the Guide for Newcomers, take the "York Quiz" found on the next five pages to see if you are a Yorker or can pass as a Yorker. The answers can be found by asking anyone who is a *real* Yorker.

YOU CAN TELL YOU'RE A YORKER IF . . .

"Scrapple" is:

1. A hard fought high school basketball game in York County.
2. That gunk you use to cover the cracks on dry wall.
3. That yuppie drink.
4. A dish made from assorted pork products.

YOU CAN TELL YOU'RE A YORKER IF . . .

"Shushly" is:

1. A move on skis at Ski Roundtop.
2. The name of the guy who made the list in that movie about the Holocaust.
3. What you say to your kids when you are trying to quiet them for bed.
4. A "Dutch" word meaning nervous or flighty.

YOU CAN TELL YOU'RE A YORKER IF . . .

A "Fengfish" is:

1. A Type of Piranha.
2. One of those little crackers that look like fish.
3. Wasn't that Dennis Fengfish who was the criminalist in the O. J. trial?
4. A good York name.

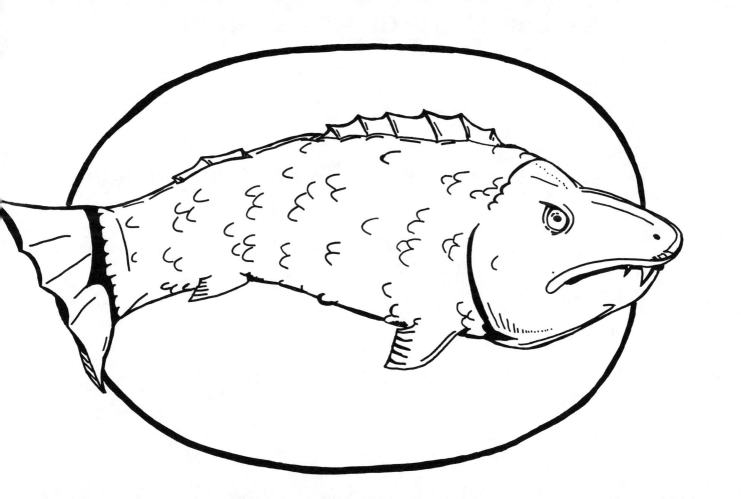

What is thrown away when butchering a hog:

1. Its brains.
2. Its stomach and intestines.
3. Its feet.
4. Its squeal.

YOU CAN TELL YOU'RE A YORKER IF . . .

"Hog Maw" is:

1. A big mouth on a very large person.
2. The mother of piglets.
3. A biker chick on a Harley.
4. A pig's stomach stuffed with meat, potatoes, and vegetables.

CONTRIBUTOR'S PAGE

Yes, I want to see my idea in print. I want to contribute to the next edition of **"You Can Tell You're A Yorker If . . ."** My idea(s) are shown below. Don't forget to give me credit.

You Can Tell You're A Yorker If . . . _____

_____

_____

You Can Tell You're A Yorker If . . . _____

_____

_____

Name: _____

Address: _____

City: _____ State: _____ Zip: _____

Telephone: (_____) _____

Mail to: Winemiller Press

2625 Winemiller Lane

York, PA 17404

ORDER FORM

 Postal Orders: Winemiller Press, 2625 Winemiller Lane, York, PA 17404
Telephone: (717) 764-1964.

Please send me _____ copies of **"YOU CAN TELL YOU'RE A YORKER IF . . . "**. I understand that I may return any books for a full refund -- for any reason, no questions asked.

Price: $6.95 **Add Shipping:** $1.75 for the 1st book, $.50 for each additional book. Pa. residents, please add 6% sales tax.

Discounts:

1 - 2	no discount
3 - 10	20%
11 - 20	30%
21 and up	40%

Payment:
❏ Check
❏ Money Order

Company name:_____

Name:_____

Address:_____

City:_____ State:_____ Zip: _____ - _____

Telephone: (_____) _____

ORDER FORM

Postal Orders: Winemiller Press, 2625 Winemiller Lane, York, PA 17404
Telephone: (717) 764-1964.

Please send me _____ copies of **"YOU CAN TELL YOU'RE A YORKER IF . . . "**. I understand that I may return any books for a full refund -- for any reason, no questions asked.

Price: $6.95 **Add Shipping:** $1.75 for the 1st book, $.50 for each additional book. Pa. residents, please add 6% sales tax.

Discounts:

			Payment:
1 - 2	no discount		❏ Check
3 - 10	20%		❏ Money Order
11 - 20	30%		
21 and up	40%		

Company name:_____

Name:_____

Address:_____

City:_____ State:_____ Zip: _____ - _____

Telephone: (_____) _____